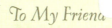
To My Friend

_____

From

_____

Date

_____

Prayers to Calm Your Heart

Elizabeth George

Artwork by

Susan Winget

H

HARVEST HOUSE PUBLISHERS
EUGENE, OREGON

Prayers to Calm Your Heart

Text copyright © 2014 by Elizabeth George

Artwork copyright © by Susan Winget

Published by Harvest House Publishers
Eugene, Oregon 97402
www.harvesthousepublishers.com

ISBN 978-0-7369-3851-8

Text is adapted from *Breaking the Worry Habit...Forever!* by Elizabeth George
(Harvest House Publishers, 2009).

The artwork of Susan Winget is used by Harvest House Publishers, Inc. under authorization from
Courtney Davis, Inc. For more information regarding art prints featured in this book, please contact:

Courtney Davis, Inc.
55 Francisco Street, Suite 450
San Francisco, California 94133
www.susanwinget.com

Design and production by Garborg Design Works, Savage, Minnesota

Printed in China

13 14 15 16 17 18 19 20 21 / LP / 10 9 8 7 6 5 4 3 2 1

With thanksgiving to my Lord,

I dedicate this book in loving memory to my cherished mother-in-law,

Lois Osgood George Onesti, a faithful woman of prayer.

She prayed for my salvation, my husband, and our children.

The answers to her prayers live on!

CONTENTS

Are You Burdened with Responsibilities?

Jesus answered and said to her,
"Martha, Martha, you are worried
and troubled about many things."

LUKE 10:41

Do you ever wake up in the morning and feel as though the weight of the world is on your shoulders...before you even get out of bed? You wonder, *Just how many people, commitments, and responsibilities can I keep in the air at the same time?* The issue is not that you aren't responsible. It's just the opposite. You are *hyper*-conscious and aware of your many roles, duties, and responsibilities! That's why life seems to be an impossible burden at times.

Married or single, you have mountains of responsibility. Responsibility is not a bad thing. It's a good thing to experience the tension of having people to see, places to go, and things to do. That's what life is made of! It keeps us going and growing, active and alive, useful and involved. But there is also a downside, especially if we mishandle the burden of responsibility.

What's the solution to worrying about your responsibilities? It centers on making two choices. First, choose to focus on God, not on your work and responsibilities. Your hectic schedule and endless to-do lists will always be a part of your day-in, day-out existence. It's a given! And even though doing your duties and faithfully living out your roles are essential, in the larger scope of the Christian life, they are not the most important things. What is vital is a closer walk with Jesus. When God is your focus—your top priority and the center of your minutes and days—you won't need to worry about your daily duties and circumstances. He will provide the wisdom you need to make right choices. And He will give you all the strength you need to endure them.

Your second must-make choice is to focus on today. Teach yourself to take one day at a time. It helps to remember Jesus' words: "Do not worry about tomorrow, for tomorrow will worry about its own things. Sufficient for the day is its own trouble" (Matthew 6:34). And what about tomorrow? No worries! Jesus will be there too—to love you, take care of you, guide you, stay beside you, and calm your anxious heart.

It helps to realize that some duties will need to be done every day you're alive. Others, however, will come and go with the seasons of your life. So focus your attention, time, and energies fully on the tasks God has for you today. Then tomorrow, ask Him what His priorities are for your life and your day. They may or may not be the same as today's priorities. And ask Him once again to equip you. This is how you break the worry habit and calm your heart—by looking at each day's responsibilities and then looking fully into God's wonderful face and moving forward in His power and grace. Then when pressure mounts, follow this path to peace:

- ∾ *Stop what you're doing*—all your busyness, all your stewing, all your doing, all your running around in circles, all your accusing and complaining.
- ∾ *Sit down*—both in body and in heart.
- ∾ *Seek God's peace and priorities*—through prayer.
- ∾ *Start again*—with a quiet heart, the right attitude, and God's right direction for your time and energy.

Dear Lord, help me focus on what's right in front of me...just for today. You are only asking me to deal with one day at a time—this day. Thank You that I don't have to worry about anything! Because You are right here beside me as I go through this day, I can face every situation with a calm heart. Then I'll do the same tomorrow.

You will keep him in perfect peace whose mind is stayed on You.

ISAIAH 26:3

9

Are You Anxious About What Could Happen?

*But when he saw that the wind
was boisterous, he was afraid.*

MATTHEW 14:30

E

A look down the corridor of the future can definitely give you much to fret about as you think about what could happen. Do you fear the loss of a job or income? Or maybe you fear the possibility of a stroke, heart attack, a serious fall suffered by yourself or a loved one, or even worse—the "Big C" (cancer). And of course, every mom fears an accident at the pool or beach or a car wreck involving one of her children.

Whatever circumstance—or potential circumstance—causes you to be anxious, in most cases it's something you can do very little, if anything, about. But think about it. You can call 911 in an emergency, set up and faithfully keep doctor appointments, and head for the shelter when a tornado is sighted, as I did often while growing up in Oklahoma. Or you can travel inland like my daughter did—twice—when a hurricane is about to slam into your area of the coast. But what about earthquakes? Our family survived two large ones while living in Southern California. And what about random acts of violence? A break-in? We've experienced each of those as well. I'm sure you have your own list of worry topics that can send your nerves into orbit.

So what can you do about all that could happen to you and your loved ones? First, realize there is a difference between concern and worry or fear. Concern moves you to prayer, to action, and to preparation. But worry and fear immobilize you. Next, learn when dealing with worry and real fear to ask and answer this question, "Where is my faith?" Faith involves trust in God, while worry is a lack of trust. Worry says, "My problems and issues are too big for even God to deal with." But trust says, "I can do all things through Christ who strengthens me" (Philippians 4:13).

Trust. We hear of trust and read about it in the Bible. If you are at all like me, just the sound and thought of "trust" makes you yearn for it in greater measure. So what are some keys to strengthening this essential element? To growing to the point where you don't waver the next time a perceived threat appears on the horizon? And how can you gain the peace of mind a solid trust in God brings to your heart?

RED KNOT

Build a close relationship with God. A friendship with the Lord will sustain you in times and situations when you might give in to worry or fear.

Count on God's Word. Spend some time each day reading your Bible to learn of God's power and faithfulness to take care of His people. As you learn more about God, you will trust Him more.

Pray about everything. Whatever you're involved in or facing head-on, whatever is happening to you at any single minute, whatever surprise or tragedy appears out of nowhere, pray! Prayer enables you to tap into God's wisdom anywhere, anytime, no matter what's going on.

Build your trust in God. Every time you turn your life issues over to God and allow Him to lead, you build trust in Him. Trust Him for wisdom...regarding your issue. Trust Him for love...for the people involved in your issue. Trust Him for a sound mind...in dealing with your issue. And trust Him for power...as you remain steadfast.

Step out in faith. Get moving! Do whatever God communicates to you. Do what you know is right. And do whatever you can to set aside worry and manage your fear-and-anxiety-producing problem.

And one last word. You may have to do this minute by minute, and certainly problem by problem. But your goal is to calm your heart when you are tempted to worry by building your trust in God and establishing the habit of prayer. Just for today—calm your heart. Refuse to worry. Do your part. Pray to God. And trust Him fully.

Father, my first thought as I look at the future and all its uncertainties is to shrink in fear. Help me not look at the unknown but at the known—the fact of Your soothing presence. Your Word tells me I can trust in You as my Good Shepherd. Whatever the future holds, I know You will be right there. That means "I shall not want" for anything.

God has not given us a spirit of fear,
but of power and of love and of a sound mind.
2 TIMOTHY 1:7

17

Are You Distressed About Making Decisions?

If any of you lacks wisdom, let him ask of God,
who gives to all liberally and without reproach,
and it will be given to him.

JAMES 1:5

I'm sure no one has to tell you about the importance of making right decisions. Your physical, social, financial, and spiritual issues need to be taken seriously. And that's a good thing! Unfortunately, we sometimes learn the most by coming to a wrong conclusion.

For instance, have you made some poor financial decisions? Hopefully now you want to be wise when it comes to shelling out money to buy a computer, a car, a home, or whatever else you are considering. If you've made some bad choices in the years gone by, now is the time to start making decisions that will help others instead of harming them.

If you can learn to take a few preliminary steps before rushing into something; or before choosing rashly or emotionally or without consideration—then you can be less worried and more confident that you're making right choices. Put this process to work for you:

- *Review each decision.* Clarify exactly what is being asked of you. Pray and review your situation before God. Ask Him for guidance and discernment. Also ask others who would know the answers or point you toward them.

- *Refine your options.* Always look for options—godly options, good, better, and best options!

- *Remember God's Word.* Get in the habit of asking yourself, "What does the Bible say about different choices and their consequences?" The Bible is your standard. If any choice doesn't agree with Scripture, you can know it's a choice to reject.

- *Restrain your emotions.* When we are upset, fearful, intimidated, mad, or sad, wrong decisions are sure to be made. If you're suffering from any of the above, put your decision making on pause. Pray until you get your emotions under control. Then approach your choices with a clear head and a heart that's calm and unclouded by feelings.

- *Re-examine your motives.* Motives are deceptive. When you get down to the business of making a decision, ask yourself, "Am I doing this or wanting this because it's the right thing to do or want...or because it's what I want?"

- *Resist impatience.* So often we're in a hurry to do or purchase something or go somewhere. This is where prayer comes to your rescue. How? Prayer makes you wait. Prayer slows you down. As you pray, you realize your dependence on God. And you're reminded of His power and provision. Prayer also reveals your motives. It searches your heart and identifies wrong motives. Prayer points you in the right direction as you begin the process of decision making and deal with doubts or an unsettled heart.

- *Respond and make the decision.* Once you've walked through this process, you should be confident that the decision you are making is a good one. Why? Because you're choosing to follow God's leading.

Each and every decision you make, regardless of its level of intensity, is vitally important as you seek to do God's will. And that's exactly what decision making is—seeking to do God's will so you live in His will. So take a deep breath. Calm your heart and clear your mind. Set aside some time to sit down...and then pray. Involve God in your choices. He will guide you.

Dear Lord, I admit I mistakenly think I'm capable of making my own decisions and fail to consult You. I can't believe I actually imagine that I know what's best for me. Help me resist the temptation to do things my way. Guide my heart to seek Your way—the best way. My desire is to please You by praying, "Not my will but Yours be done!"

Be anxious for nothing, but in everything
by prayer and supplication, with thanksgiving,
let your requests be made known to God;
and the peace of God, which surpasses all understanding,
will guard your hearts and minds through Christ Jesus.

PHILIPPIANS 4:6-7

Are You Troubled About Your Family?

The LORD will give strength to His people;
The LORD will bless His people with peace.

PSALM 29:11

Worrying about the health and well-being of family members comes with being a part of a family. But try this. Turn your worries for your spouse, your children, and your parents into opportunities to trust God. Think of ways to help them. Concentrate on doing your part to honor and care for your parents. Focus on respecting and helping your spouse. Diligently train and protect your children. This focus on the family calls for a decision, a commitment, and lots of love and effort...for a long time.

ARE YOU WORRIED ABOUT YOUR HUSBAND?

Therefore a man shall leave his father and mother
and be joined to his wife,
and they shall become one flesh.

GENESIS 2:24

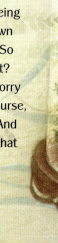

As a married woman, my closest friend and companion is my husband. Together Jim and I traveled through the beginnings of a fresh young marriage and experienced the addition of children, seeing them grow up, marry, and begin their own families. This was all natural and good. So today, who's left at home to worry about? Who's Number One on my "People to Worry About" list? Why, it's my husband, of course, the other part of the team I belong to! And if you're married, you know all too well that there is plenty to worry about, like...

- *Health issues.* These are at the top of most wives' list of concerns in a marriage. With the passage of time, real and potential health problems probably will surface, aches and pains are sure to crop up, and conditions eventually develop that signal it's time for an altered lifestyle.

- *Job issues.* At one time or another, everyone who has a job wonders and worries about the security of their personal job or their spouse's employment. And on-the-job stress is another very real concern.

- *Spiritual issues.* When it comes to your spouse's spiritual growth—or lack of it—well, it can be a stress and worry producer.

- *Fidelity issues.* Sexual temptation in marriage certainly isn't new...nor is a wife's temptation to worry about it.

- *Friendship issues.* Both partners must work at having fun and finding common interests for a marriage to be an alive and vibrant relationship. But with demanding jobs, a house full of kids, grandkids, activities, commitments, friends, parents, and in-laws, it's easy to see how distance can develop in a marriage.

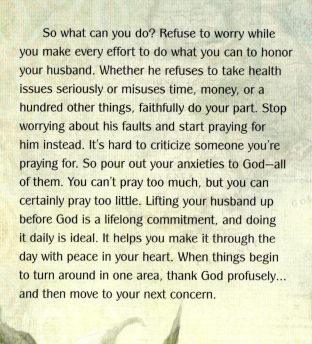

So what can you do? Refuse to worry while you make every effort to do what you can to honor your husband. Whether he refuses to take health issues seriously or misuses time, money, or a hundred other things, faithfully do your part. Stop worrying about his faults and start praying for him instead. It's hard to criticize someone you're praying for. So pour out your anxieties to God—all of them. You can't pray too much, but you can certainly pray too little. Lifting your husband up before God is a lifelong commitment, and doing it daily is ideal. It helps you make it through the day with peace in your heart. When things begin to turn around in one area, thank God profusely... and then move to your next concern.

L'ITALIE
DIVISÉE EN
SES ESTATS

Are You Worried About Your Children?

Train up a child in the way he should go.

PROVERBS 22:6

It's hard not to worry about the well-being of your children...and grandchildren. Of course you do your best to protect them, but it's also true that you can't keep them sheltered at home forever.

As parents—and now grandparents—Jim and I have gone through the birth of a grandchild with a physical defect and the ensuing corrective surgery and treatment, the hospitalization

30

of another grandchild in an emergency situation, and a daughter's bout with a malignant tumor and all that entails. Each one of these crises was utterly alarming. Each one was fertile soil for sickening worry. Yet each one forced me to do battle with worry and press myself closer to God through prayer. And, to God's glory, each one grew in me a greater trust in God's plan and a fuller understanding of His promised love and care for me *and* my afflicted family members. These assurances, remembered in prayer, never fail to calm my anxious heart.

Legitimate concern will always be part of the very nature of a mom. After all, looking out for our kids is one of our responsibilities and assignments from God. He wants us to be like the mother who "watches over the ways of her household" (Proverbs 31:27)—and that includes the children. But as a mom, you need to remember that a loving and compassionate God is one hundred percent aware of your child's situation. That means you can cease all your worrying and count on God. Sure, you are to be diligent and faithful to do your part. But you are to just as diligently and faithfully trust God for His part. Rather than worry, choose to pray and place your children's physical safety into the loving hands of God.

Are you worried about your children's behavior, their social, financial, or marital status, or their circle of friends? Are you concerned about their spiritual condition? When you are, take action and...

- *pray for your children.* Pray faithfully for their character and choices. Dear mom, never forget that "the effective, fervent prayer of a righteous man (or mom) avails much" (James 5:16).

- *be available for your children.* Make a point of being near or with them often, so they know you are available whenever they need you.

- *prepare your children.* Faithfully instruct them from God's Word. The Bible is the ultimate book of wisdom and advice. It's full of information about the dangers of being in the wrong places or with the wrong people, about good habits, and about sexual purity. Help your children understand God's love and care and His presence.

- *guard your children.* God has given your children to you! And He's assigned you to watch over, instruct, and train them. Be faithful to your long-term responsibility to provide strong parental leadership.

If you're worried about your children, try a new tactic and do something about it. Turn fully to God...and pray. If you're unsure of what to pray, open your heart and simply ask, "Lord, what do You want me to do?" (Acts 9:6).

ARE YOU WORRIED ABOUT YOUR AGING PARENTS?

Honor your father and your mother.

EXODUS 20:12

Most women are deeply concerned about their parents' welfare. This is a good thing, but it usually means we tend to worry about our parents. And if we're married, we also take on the task of worrying for the welfare of our in-laws.

Hopefully you are deeply involved in your parents' lives. You know what's happening or not happening with them. You show love and respect by checking up on them often. This is the way it should be. But without the worry! Worry is of no benefit to you or your parents, and it will have no positive effect on any of you.

What's the best way to deal with your concerns? Be involved in your parents' lives. God asks and expects you to care about, care for, and love them. During the years and decades that your parents are in good health, focus on feeding the fires of love for them. Then when the time comes and you are needed, your heart will be ready to spring into action. In the meantime,

∽ *spend time with your parents.* If your parents are close by, schedule regular times to get together. If they live some distance away, plan in advance to make this happen.

∽ *stay in touch with your parents.* Call, email, write, text, Skype, Facebook—whatever it takes!—your parents often. Figure out as many ways as you can to keep up to date...and do it.

∽ *pray for your parents.* You cannot neglect—or hate—the person you are praying for. Let prayer pave the way for loving family relationships.

Dear Lord, how I thank You for my family! I am blessed beyond measure. As a daughter, wife, and mother, You have given me people to love and care for. Help me honor my parents and in-laws, support my husband, and serve my children. Give me a fierce love for my family. Calm my heart as I trust You for the safety and well-being of my precious loved ones.

Now may the Lord of peace Himself give you peace always in every way. The Lord be with you.

2 Thessalonians 3:16

37

N
E
S

Tortoise

0   Miles

0   Kms.

10   Miles   0

Are You Worried About Your Health?

*Who of you by being worried
can add a single hour to his life?*

Matthew 6:27 nasb

There are certain red-letter days in every woman's life. The memory of one of mine—and recalling the anxiety that arrived with it—will never go away. It all began with a routine exam. The look on my doctor's face when she said, "I don't like the look of things," caused me to stare at the floor and not want to hear any more. Although in time everything worked out well due to surgery and God's abundant grace, I went through a serious bout with worry, fear, anxiety, and speculation.

Health issues are fertile soil for the all-too-easy-to-cultivate habit of worry. I know, and I speak from experience as I moved rapidly toward the "Worrywart of the Year" award. I had to put a halt to my worrying. I had to regroup, retrain, and move out in an entirely different direction—the right direction—so I could know and live with the peace only God can provide when I trusted Him with all my heart.

Have you ever heard the saying, "The moment you are born, you begin to die"? Life and health are gifts from God. So what can you do when you suffer? Let these truths from God's Word calm your heart.

~ *Your life is not guaranteed to be free of pain or illness.* When sin entered the world, so did pain, disease, illness, and death. Jesus said, "In the world you will have tribulation" (John 16:33). No matter what pain you face, you can bring calm to your heart by praying and looking heavenward to the day when "God will wipe away every tear from their eyes; there shall be no more death, nor sorrow, nor crying. There shall be no more pain, for the former things have passed away" (Revelation 21:4).

~ *Your physical pain is an opportunity to trust God.* The apostle Paul had a painful, lingering condition, which he referred to as his "thorn in the flesh." As he struggled with it, he prayed to God and asked Him to take it away. What was God's answer? God calmed Paul's heart by promising him, "My grace is sufficient for you, for My strength is made perfect

in weakness" (2 Corinthians 12:9). The Lord assured Paul that even though he was suffering, he—Paul—was not alone. God was with him, strengthening him. When you suffer, it is always an opportunity to trust God. And as you trust Him, you rest in Him...which brings you peace of mind and soul.

Your spiritual health is more important than physical health. As much as you and I value our good health, when we became Christians, our physical life took a backseat to our spiritual life. Therefore focus beyond your pain. Embrace and nurture a heavenly perspective. "For our citizenship is in heaven, from which we also eagerly wait for the Savior, the Lord Jesus Christ, who will transform our lowly body that it may be conformed to His glorious body" (Philippians 3:20-21).

Your life and health are important. However, they are temporary and earthly. As a child of God, you are moving day by day toward a better existence, one that is glorious, eternal, and heavenly. But while you are here, be a good steward of the body God has given you for His work here on earth. And don't worry about it. Instead pray as you do what you can to take care of your body.

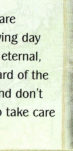

- Eat foods that are nutritious and healthful.
- Exercise regularly. Every little bit helps!
- Attend regular checkups with your doctor.
- Follow up on any warning signs.
- Keep your focus on heaven. Looking up keeps your mind in the right place.
- Trust in the wisdom of God. He knows what He's doing.

Worry can definitely take your eyes off God. Worry says that this—whatever "this" is that you're worrying about—is something that can't be handled by God, with God, or by His grace. Your goal is to stop worrying! Exchange the bad habit of worrying with the excellent habit of trusting God. Whatever your situation, take time to pray and turn your concern over to God. You'll be glad you did!

God, when I'm in good health, remind me to give thanks instead of assuming that good health will last forever. When I'm in poor or failing health, help me to give thanks, knowing that You, the Great Physician, have my best in mind. May You be glorified in whatever conditions and circumstances I find myself. Remind me that I am always and forever under Your ever-present care.

Blessed are all those who put their trust in Him.

PSALM 2:12

Are You Fretful About Your Finances?

I have learned in whatever state I am, to be content:
I know how to be abased, and I know how to abound.

PHILIPPIANS 4:11-12

Ever since Adam and Eve were forced
out of the Garden of Eden, mankind has faced
a big daily problem—finding and providing
food, clothing, and shelter. And that can be
a common cause for worry because they all
require money. I've had my own bouts with
financial trials. I remember all too well some
serious struggles...when Jim and I were
newlyweds attending college without financial
support, when we moved from Tennessee
to Los Angeles where the cost of living was
four times higher, and when we lived as a

family of four on a severely reduced income because Jim quit his job to go to seminary. That was then. And now? I still wake up in the night with my mind running wild, tempted to fret about not only the present but the future too.

Jesus told His followers, "Do not worry about your life, what you will eat or what you will drink: nor about your body, what you will put on" (Matthew 6:25). His message is crystal clear. It's to the point. And it is delivered in three simple, understandable words: *Do not worry.*

If you read Jesus' entire message in Matthew 6:25-34, you'll discover some key reasons why you don't need to worry, and why you can trust God and count on Him to oversee every detail of your life. For instance,

- *you are valuable to God (verse 26).*
- *your situation is under God's control, not yours (verse 27).*
- *you will—will—be taken care of (verse 28-30).*
- *your every need is known to God (verses 31-32).*

When life gets tough, you can choose to look up and count on God's forever promises. With a clear head and a trusting heart, you can put aside worrying and do something about the problem. When money is tight, scarce...or even nonexistent, put your time, anxiety, and fears to work in a positive way.

- *First and foremost, keep your head and your heart in God's Word.* Between the covers of your Bible, you'll find encouragement while you suffer, instruction about how to endure, promises to cling to and trust, truth about God's love, and facts about His total ability to take care of His people, including you.
- *Pray.* When you pray, you're following God's pattern for a quiet heart. Make a decision to catch yourself when you start worrying about finances and pray instead.

- *Get help.* Talk to someone in your church or community who can give you good, sound financial advice. Check out a budget book from your public library. Download free books. Take a class on managing money. Do something to get help.

- *Cut back.* Put the brakes on accumulating things or services you don't need. If possible, do the work yourself. Opportunities to cut back are everywhere...if you're looking for them.

- *Learn to be content.* As the verse for this reading states, contentment is learned through circumstances and trials. God is your wonderful helper, and He's always standing by you. He never fails to supply all you need to endure. So be content!

But how about the opposite scenario? Let's say you have the good job, the great salary, the dream house, new car, and exciting lifestyle—with, of course, the funds to finance it. Ambition and industry are excellent qualities...and earning a high income through commitment, dedication, and good hard work is noble. But then what?

Within eight years of marriage, Jim and I had all this. There we were, stuffing our lives full of stuff, and still we were restless. We couldn't shake the emptiness. Well, I can only praise God for His intervention in our lives. By His grace I responded to God's message of salvation, Jim renewed his commitment to Christ, and our perspective on our possessions was permanently altered.

The word "possession" means something owned, occupied, or controlled. The issue for you and me is not whether we own something. It's whether we can let go of it! People worry about their things because acquiring them is often a major life goal. So we worry about *not* having them. Then we worry about *how* to get them. Then once we have them, we worry about *keeping* them. No, having more does not bring contentment.

So what is the usefulness of money and possessions? It's to bless others! To help others. To better others. To support others. If God has blessed you and your family with finances and possessions, praise Him heartily! Then take every opportunity to share it with others.

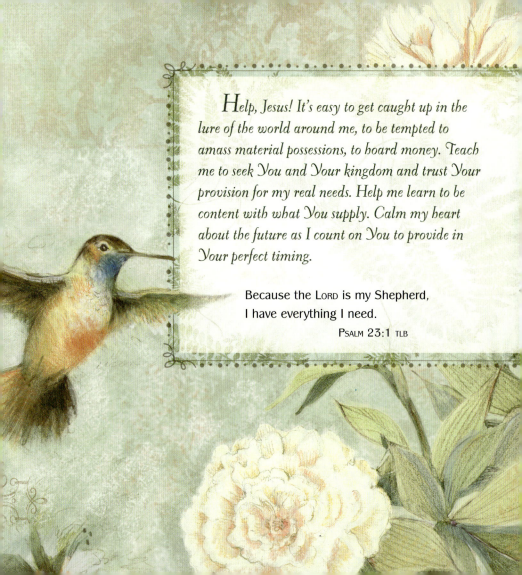

Help, Jesus! It's easy to get caught up in the lure of the world around me, to be tempted to amass material possessions, to hoard money. Teach me to seek You and Your kingdom and trust Your provision for my real needs. Help me learn to be content with what You supply. Calm my heart about the future as I count on You to provide in Your perfect timing.

Because the Lord is my Shepherd,
I have everything I need.

PSALM 23:1 TLB

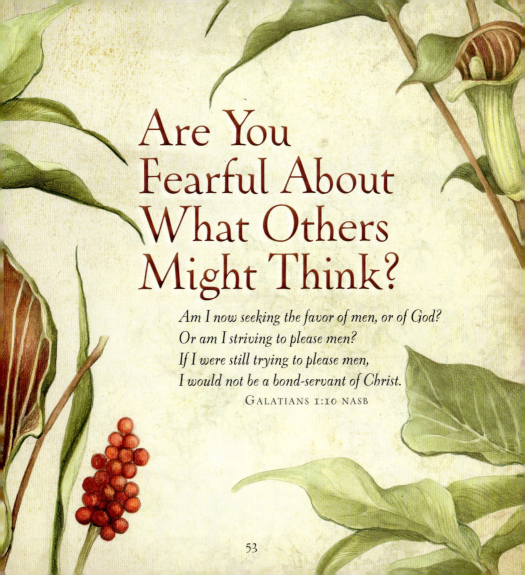

Are You Fearful About What Others Might Think?

Am I now seeking the favor of men, or of God?
Or am I striving to please men?
If I were still trying to please men,
I would not be a bond-servant of Christ.

GALATIANS 1:10 NASB

I don't know where your weak spot is when it comes to desiring the approval and acceptance of others, but I do know that no one is immune from it. And it's a hindrance to spiritual growth and usefulness. It can lead us to compromise our beliefs and principles for the approval of others. It can cause us to sit on the sidelines in fear of what others will think, or how we will be judged. It can keep us from stepping out in obedience or speaking up in fear of what it might do to our reputation.

I grew up under the umbrella of "What will others think?" Whenever I did something foolish, I was confronted with that question. Even if what I did was good (having a job while attending college versus not having one, taking summer school classes instead of going home for the summer, waiting to have children versus starting a family right away), it was always the same question. "What will others think?"

So how do you avoid the mental anguish and anxiety that comes with the urge to give in to peer pressure or the fear of rejection or being harassed? It's not easy, but there is hope and help. Others have broken this habit of needing approval, and so can you! Here are some things you can do, as always with God's help.

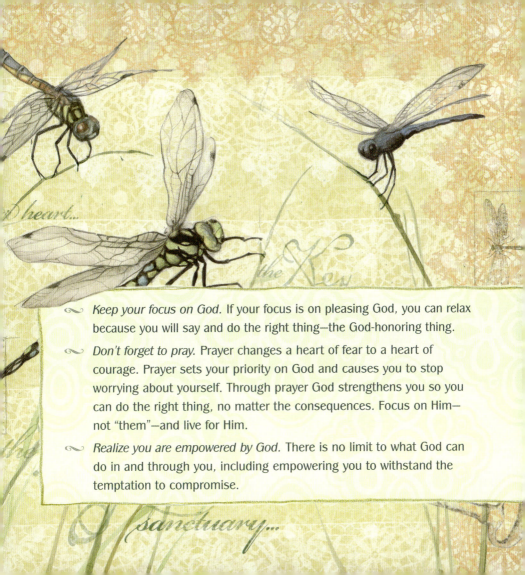

- *Keep your focus on God.* If your focus is on pleasing God, you can relax because you will say and do the right thing—the God-honoring thing.

- *Don't forget to pray.* Prayer changes a heart of fear to a heart of courage. Prayer sets your priority on God and causes you to stop worrying about yourself. Through prayer God strengthens you so you can do the right thing, no matter the consequences. Focus on Him— not "them"—and live for Him.

- *Realize you are empowered by God.* There is no limit to what God can do in and through you, including empowering you to withstand the temptation to compromise.

God created you as a social being. Maybe that is why we stew so much about our relationships. It's natural to not want to be alone. And you don't want to be left out. You want friends, and you want to belong.

But God wants you to keep tight reins on your desire to belong and have the approval of others. Ask yourself, "Are my desires for approval turning me away from God and from following Him?" If Jesus is your Savior, He is also your friend. Seek His favor above all others. Realize that in Jesus you will always have at least one friend, the best of all friends, the ultimate friend. Even if everyone else turns away from you, you can know peace in your heart. God is there.

And He promises He will never leave you or forsake you (Hebrews 13:5).

Heavenly Father, help me remember to ask, "Am I seeking the approval of others with my actions, or am I seeking Your approval?" Obviously Your satisfaction should be my first and foremost thought in each and every action. My desire is to stand before You one day and hear You say, "Well done, good and faithful servant." Prod me to live each day with this goal in mind.

The LORD is my helper; I will not fear. What can man do to me?

HEBREWS 13:6

Are You Overwhelmed by Sin?

I acknowledged my sin to You,
and my iniquity I have not hidden.
I said, "I will confess my transgressions to the LORD."
PSALM 32:5

Guilt over sin is definitely a life issue Christians need to be concerned about. Whenever we offend God's holy character (which is sin), we should be *deeply* concerned. And whenever we're holding on to a sin or a sinful practice and refusing to acknowledge it and give it up, we should care profoundly!

Be thankful God has given you a conscience. It's that inner voice that reminds you when you've done something wrong. It's the prick of conviction that leads you to do the right thing and walk in God's ways.

How does a slide into sin begin? It often starts with a mere second glance or a second thought, with a question or a hesitation. Then rationalization can set in to convince you that the option in front of you is something you not only want, but something you think you need...and even deserve! When you reach this point, you're usually a goner, and the battle against temptation is lost. To fight this battle, put these tactics to use:

- *Be aware of sin's consequences.* Committing an offense against God spawns guilt and shame, even leading you to try to hide what you did...and try to hide from God. If you are running from God, it's best to give it up now. God loves you! And He's waiting to hear you pray, to welcome you, to celebrate your return. Run to Him now. His forgiveness and peace will be yours.

- *Be quick to acknowledge your transgressions.* The worst step you can take when you slip up and fail to follow God's ways is to try to blame others or rationalize the cause or seriousness of your failure. When you sin, you're guilty, whether you own your actions or not. So confess your transgressions as soon as possible.

Figure 1   Figure 2   Figure 3   Figure 4

Figure 5   Figure 6   Figure 7   Figure 8   Figure 9

∽ *Make it a habit to keep a short account with God.* When you sin, rush to confess it. You can do it in a split second. Just say, "Oh, Lord, that was so wrong! Forgive me."

∽ *Choose to steer clear of situations that may cause you to stumble.* Be aware of the effects of your surroundings. If there are people in your path who tempt you away from the things of God, avoid them and choose other friends. Also stay away from the places that entice you to sin. Only fools rush in where angels fear to tread!

Praise God He forgives you when you confess and repent. As you bring your guilty conscience to God, acknowledge your wrongdoing, and agree with Him that what you've done is unacceptable, He is faithful to continually remove your sin and guilt (see 1 John 1:9).

To enjoy days filled with peace of mind, pray often. Regularly turn over every concern to God. Capture the energy you lose to fits of worry and anxiety, and use it to focus on helping others. Break free from your worries and serve God with all your heart. Pray about everything, about all things. Your Father in heaven will calm your heart, and bless you with His peace. Look to God day by day. Pray to Him. He will hear you. And He is ready, willing, and able to encourage you.

It's me, Lord, once again overwhelmed by Your goodness. Truly, Your loving-kindness endures forever. I come to You with a repentant heart, knowing that in Jesus You have removed my sins—as far as the east is from the west. My heart is calm, resting in the knowledge that all is forgiven, that I am burden-free, that all is well with my soul. Thank You!

Let us therefore come boldly to the throne
of grace, that we may obtain mercy and find
grace to help in time of need.

HEBREWS 4:16